A Short History of France for Teens and Exchange Students

David B. McCoy

Spare Change Press™
Massillon, Ohio

Proofreaders: Mary Ann D'Aurelio, Dr. Rhonda Baughman,
and the host of *The French History* Podcast,
Gary Girod.

Cover painting: *The Republic, sketch for the contest of 1848* by Alexandre-Marie Colin. See page 34.

Spare Change Press™
Massillon, Ohio
sparechangepress79@gmail.com

SpareChangePress.com
amazon.com/author/davidmccoy

To my son, Brian, who now calls France “home.”

A Short History of France

At least 70,000 years ago, the first people to inhabit France were stone-age hunters, the Neanderthals. Short, stocky, and physically strong, they were hunter-gatherers who used tools made of stone and animal bones. Sometime between 40,000 and 30,000 BCE, another race of humans, Cro-Magnons, arrived in France. Like the Neanderthals, the Cro-Magnons were hunter-gatherers who roamed from place to place, following migrating herds. However, the Cro-Magnons were more advanced and efficient hunters who regularly stalked and killed large beasts, including mammoths, reindeer, and horses.

Lascaux animals

The Cro-Magnons also produced art in the form of cave paintings. The most impressive known examples were discovered in 1940 at Lascaux in the Aquitaine region. When archaeologists explored the site, they found more than 600 paintings and almost 1,500 engravings carved into the walls. The cave was open to the public in 1948, but was closed in 1963 because visitors' breath and body heat were damaging the paintings. In 1983, an exact replica of the cave and its artworks, Lascaux II, opened near Montignac, France.

The hunter-gatherer societies living in France changed very little for thousands of years. Then, about 4000 BCE, new nomadic tribes arrived in the area, bringing with them knowledge of how to grow crops and raise livestock. Combined with hunting, this knowledge provided people with a much more reliable food supply allowing them to settle down and create farms and villages.

Between 1000 and 750 BCE, tribes of people calling themselves Celts migrated into France from central Europe. The Celts were considerably more advanced than the natives already inhabiting the area. Unearthed Celtic tombs reveal an impressive culture of material possessions. One tomb discovered at Vix in Burgundy contained a four-wheeled Chariot, many items of personal property, and a superb golden diadem. (A diadem is a type of crown, specifically an ornamental headband worn by monarchs.)

Detail from a La Tene Cauldron

The La Tene Celts (on the northern side of Lake Neuchâtel in Switzerland) are synonymous with advanced forms of metalwork, including goldsmithing, jewelry and other decorative works. While not comparable in range with Greek art or Egyptian civilization, their works nevertheless represent a high point in Celtic design and creativity.

These Celtic Gauls, armed with formable iron-based weapons, were fearsome warriors. Exposing their tattooed bodies, they fought naked, often decapitating their victims and hanging the severed heads from their horses' manes. Ancient texts claim the heads of the most powerful enemies were embalmed. Réjane Roure of Paul Valéry University of Montpellier states, "Maybe that was to be able to say 'see that face, it was some big warrior'" (Smithsonian.com, 11, 12, 2018).

The Celts attached great importance to religious and spiritual life. They worshipped an earth goddess and a number of other deities. They also made a cult of ancestors, whom they worshipped in sanctuaries where they practiced ritual sacrifice of humans and animals.

The religious and daily life of the people were in the hands of the Druids. Druids were members of the high-ranking professional class in ancient Celtic cultures, perhaps best remembered as religious leaders, settlers of disputes, lore keepers, medical professionals, and political advisors. While the Druids are reported to have been literate, they are believed to have been prevented by tradition from recording their knowledge in written form, thus they left no written accounts of themselves.

In some year about 600 BCE, a small fleet of seagoing vessels propelled primarily by oars from the Greek city of Phocaea rowed its way into the western Mediterranean. Once there, they established a town (now known as Marseilles) with the temples, market-place, walls, magistrates, and general customs of a genuine Greek city. The Phoenicians, who already commercially controlled these waters, frowned on the intruders and did their best to drive them away. This opposition was in vain. The settlement became rooted, prospered, and defied its Canaanite competitors.

The tribesmen with whom the Greeks traded were Celts of Southern France. Stimulating trade along a network of routes made available to the Celts goods of the more advanced societies of the Near East (a transcontinental region centered on Western Asia, Turkey and Egypt.) Mediterranean luxury goods such as jewelry, decorative wears, and wine were exchanged for tin, copper, iron, cereals, salt, and slaves.

This exchange of goods helped trigger early Celtic development as grouped settlements, in most cases too small and undifferentiated to classify as towns, made their appearances. However, in the south, fortified settlements were built on high land, and some of these became major centers.

Before the Romans entered the land, there were already signs of a higher order of things. Clans were merging into confederacies covering considerable districts. Certain chiefs and tribes were striking coins with crude legends in the Greek alphabet. Left to themselves, in other words, these "Gallic" sections of the Celts might have evolved a real civilization in a few hundred years — if they had been left alone.

They were not to be left alone. Shortly before the start of the 1st century BCE, Romans began moving into France. They referred to the region as “Gaul” and called the Celts “Gauls.” Unlike the scattered Gallic (Celtic) tribes, who had no central government or national army, Rome was a well-organized nation with a large and efficient army. In 118, Romans established a colony on France’s southern coast.

Soon, the Roman colony expanded into the large province, Narbonensis. The Roman intrusion into Gaul became a full-blown conquest in 58 BCE when renowned Roman leader, Julius Caesar, marched northward from Narbonensis. Over the next eight years, Caesar subdued Gallic tribes one by one, laying waste to villages, farms, and entire cultures.

Vercingetorix

By the end of 53 BCE, Julius Caesar thought his conquest of Gaul was over, but he was wrong. In early 52, the shrewd and capable Gallic military leader, Vercingetorix, organized warriors from many tribes and fought the Roman armies to a standstill. However, he was forced to surrender when most of his allies abandoned his cause. Yet, Vercingetorix's courage has never been forgotten, and he remains a national hero with many statues erected in his name.

After conquering Gaul, the Romans began "Romanizing" the entire region. They taught the Gauls to speak Latin and to adopt Roman culture and ideas, including concepts of law and government. Over time, thousands of Romans settled in Gaul and intermarried with the Celts. They divided the country into several new provinces and built cities, roads, aqueducts, temples, amphitheaters, and bathhouses. Roman ideas and customs firmly took root and profoundly shaped the development of French culture.

For several centuries, Gaul thrived as part of the Roman Empire. In the 5th century CE, however, that empire fell apart as numerous nomadic tribes, such as the Visigoths, Vandals, Burgundians, and Franks passed through or settled Gaul. The Franks had been a loose confederacy of Germanic tribes on the right bank of the Rhine since the 3rd century. They had occasionally fought against the Romans; more often they had been their well-paid allies and had sent their warriors into Caesars' armies as mercenaries. For a long time they showed no great wish to invade Gaul. Then in the 5th century they gradually began to spread into what is now the extreme north of France. It was a slow, somewhat hesitant invasion, for the Franks were disunited.

The dominant group, the Salian Franks, were ruled by the Merovingian dynasty, who derived from the half-mythical Merowech. Nothing definite is known of Merovech's life, but an early myth made him the son of a sea god. Merowech's grandson, Clovis, king from 481 to 511 CE, laid the foundations of the Frankish state in the series of bloody campaigns. In 486, he defeated Syagrius, commander of the last outpost of the Roman Empire, and went on to defeat other barbarian rulers including the Burgundians in 500 CE and the Visigoths in 507.

When Clovis converted to Catholicism in 507 CE, the realm became Christian and has remained so ever since. He made Paris his capital city, helping to establish its long-term importance. When Clovis died in 511 CE, his kingdom was divided among his four sons. They, and the leaders of the next several generations of Merovingians, lived in a state of continuous civil wars—each attempting to gain control of the whole country for himself.

By the late 600s and early 700s, the Merovingian rulers had become so incompetent and weak they lost the reins of power to their chief advisers commonly known as the "mayors of the palace." By and large, the advisers were of what would be known as the Carolingians, and seized control of the Merovingian dynasty. In 732 CE, the Carolingian named Charles Martel saved France, when he defeated the Muslims at the Battle of Poitiers in 732. After the death of Mohammad in 632, his followers surged in all directions from their Arabian heartland. Within a century, they had spread from Palestine, along North Africa, across the Strait of Gibraltar, over the Pyrenees, to the southern border of Aquitaine. Twice the tiny Aquitanian army tried to stop their advance, but in 732 the Arab forces crossed the River Garonne and headed north for Poitiers. Immortalized by Frankish historian as the Battle of Tours, Charles's well-planned attack forced the Muslim advance back to the southern border of Aquitaine. This victory proved to be the high-water mark of the Arab invasion into Europe from their Spanish base, and earned Charles his surname Martel meaning "the hammer."

Martel's grandson, Charlemagne, engaged in even more ambitious military campaigns. In the Saxon Wars, spanning thirty years and eighteen battles, he conquered Saxonia and proceeded to convert it to Christianity. His rule also spurred the Carolingian Renaissance, a period of energetic cultural, religious, and intellectual activity within the Western Church.

Charlemagne, The Father of Europe

In only a few years, he secured an empire that included not only France, but also parts of what are now Belgium, Germany, and Italy. In the year 800 CE, Pope Leo II crowned Charlemagne Holy Roman Emperor. For this, he is often called the "Father of Europe," as he united most of Western Europe for the first time since the classical era of the Roman Empire. After Charlemagne died in 814, his descendants fought among themselves, as Clovis' heirs had. They carved the empire up into their own petty kingdoms, and it slowly fell apart. Despite this, all Holy Roman Emperors considered their kingdoms to be descendants of Charlemagne's empire, as did the French and German monarchies.

During the reign of one of the last Carolingian rulers, Charles the Simple, the seeds of a long rivalry between France and England were planted. Bands of Norsemen (Vikings) from what are now Norway and Denmark had long been raiding northern France. Eventually, the Norsemen sailed up the Seine River and attacked Paris. In 911 CE, the frightened Charles made a deal with their ruler, Rollo, giving him the region in Northwest France that was and still is called Normandy. Its people subsequently became known as Normans.

In the years that followed, the Normans transformed their small territory into a prosperous and powerful state. Within a short span of time, they became thoroughly naturalized Frenchmen in their manners, language, and institutions. They were also Christianized, and they ruled their province admirably.

Although it was physically part of France, it became more or less a separate kingdom in its own right. In 1066 CE, a descendant of Rollo, William I, crossed the English Channel, defeated the English at the battle of Hastings, and seized control of England. This earned him the nickname "William the Conqueror." The Norman-English rulers who succeeded him held onto their land in Normandy and even expanded it at the expense of French kings.

In 987 CE, the last of the enfeebled Carolingian kings died in an accident. For a century prior, the descendants of Charlemagne had actually occupied the throne only intermittently, alternating with members of the house of Robert the Strong, who were sometimes known as the Dukes of France. This family owned more land than the Carolingian kings, and its lineage were of stronger fiber. Thus, it was one of

them, Hugh Capet, who in 987 was elected by the great nobles of the land to be the sole king of the realm. The kingdom he acquired was by then a loose assemblage of discordant fragments, pieced together in the dark shadows of external pressures and internal strife. In the absence of any central authority, and roaming marauding and lawless forces, society was reduced to a condition where those who were strong protected those who were weak. Such personal relationships developed into the system of feudalism, which in the end bound the king, members of the church, knights and workmen (peasants) in an intricate web of obligations and payments. Simply put, feudalism was political and social organization reduced to the lowest terms.

The struggle of the French monarchy to overcome the contesting and divisive elements of the feudal order briefly summarizes the history of France for centuries to come. For almost nine of those centuries, following the accession of Hugh, the House of Capet, the Capetians and its cadet branches, the Valois and the Bourbons, would provide the kings under which modern France would take a lasting form. The great, consolidating achievement of the Capetians was to establish the rule of primogeniture, the right of succession belonging to the firstborn child. This did away with the tradition of dividing a kingdom among all male offspring upon the death of a king. This not only put an end to civil wars for control of the royal lands, it also created direct, or unbroken, lines of succession.

In 1137, Eleanor, daughter of William of Aquitaine, married France's Capetian crown prince, Louis. Later that year, he became King Louis VII. Eleanor's dowry included what today amounts to the southwestern quarter of France. After being divorced 15 years later by Louis, Eleanor married Henry Plantagenet, Duke of Normandy and count of Anjou, who in 1154 became King of England. This resulted in her reclaimed dowry lands being added to Henry's, which included not only England, but Normandy. Over time, the Angevin Empire was a collection of states ruled by the Angevin Plantagenet dynasty. The Plantagenets, Henry II, Richard I, and John, ruled over roughly half of medieval France as well as all of England and Ireland during the 12th and early 13th centuries. The name Angevin came from the French region and town of Anjou which was the home of the Plantagenet family.

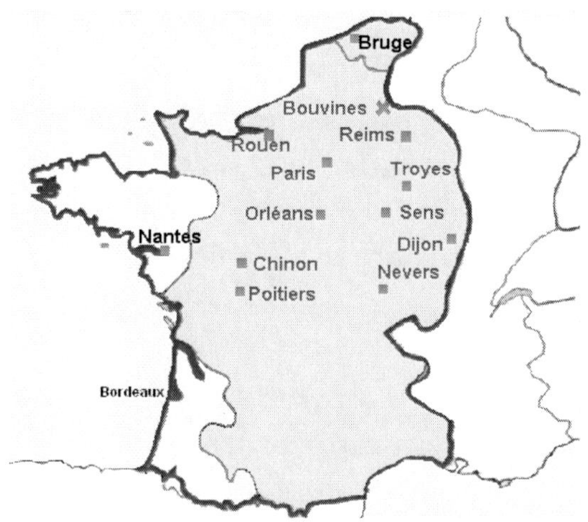

In the Battle of Bouvines, July 1214, Philip Augustus (seventh of the fourteen Capetian rulers) defeated Otto IV of Germany and the count of Flanders so decisively that Otto was deposed and replaced by Frederick II Hohenstaufen. Philip was himself able to take undisputed control of the territories of Anjou, Brittany, Maine, Normandy, and the Touraine, which he had recently seized from Otto's Angevin ally, the youngest brother of King Richard I, John I of England.

With Paris as his capital, Philip Augustus had the chief streets of Paris paved, which was a very great improvement over the dirt and mud streets so rutted, carts could hardly pass through them. He built colleges, hospitals, waterworks, walls around part of the city for defense, and the construction of the Louvre.

The Louvre has been a fixture in Paris since the late 12th century when it was built as a fortress on the banks of the Seine by Philip who wanted to protect the city from the Anglo-Normans (Vikings). In 1682, Louis XIV moved the royal residence to Versailles, and over the centuries, the Louvre fortress underwent extensive renovations and was transformed into a grand palace. Following the revolution, the Assemblée Nationale decided the Louvre would be used for displaying art and opened in 1793. In the 1980s, an extensive modernization project was undertaken with architect I.M. Pei at the helm. Nineteen eighty-nine saw the opening of the glass pyramid which is now the impressive focal point of the building's modern entrance.

Philip also continued the construction of the Catholic cathedral, Notre-Dame. The construction began in the spring 1163 with the laying of the cornerstone in the presence of King Louis VII.

Notre-Dame is a prime example of Gothic architecture which originated in 12th century France. The style was widely used, especially for cathedrals and churches, until the 16th century. The Gothic style's most prominent features included the use of the rib vault and the flying buttress, which allowed the weight of the roof to be counterbalanced by buttresses outside the building, giving greater height and more space for windows.

Another important feature was the extensive use of stained glass, and the rose window, to bring light and color to the interior. A third feature was the use of realistic statuary on the exterior, particularly over the portals, to illustrate biblical stories for the largely illiterate parishioners.

Notre Dame is one of the most widely recognized symbols of the city of Paris and the French nation. In 1905, the cathedral officially became the property of the French state rather than the Catholic Church in a move towards the secularization of France. While undergoing renovation and restoration, the roof of Notre-Dame caught fire on the evening of April 15, 2019. Burning for around 15 hours, the cathedral sustained serious damage, including the destruction of the timber spire over the crossing and most of the lead-covered wooden roof above the stone vaulted ceiling.

The Capetians, unable to produce a male heir, were succeeded in 1328 by the Valois Dynasty. As a result, King Edward III of England believed that the reigning French King, Philip VI, held the throne illegitimately. He argued he could legally claim the French throne through a line of descent via his mother, Isabella of France. Edward, thus, declared himself King of France and invaded, resulting in the devastating Hundred Years' War.

The Hundred Years' War was fought between France and England over the French throne from 1337 to 1453 (which, as you can see, was in fact longer than 100 years). Also, the war was not fought continuously but in phases. Initially England dominated the fighting, but the tide of war would in time turn in France's favor. By 1453, the French throne was secured by the House of Valois (a cadet branch of the extinct House of Capet), while all English possessions in France, with the exception of Calais, were lost. What follows are summaries of the five most significant battles of the Hundred Years' War.

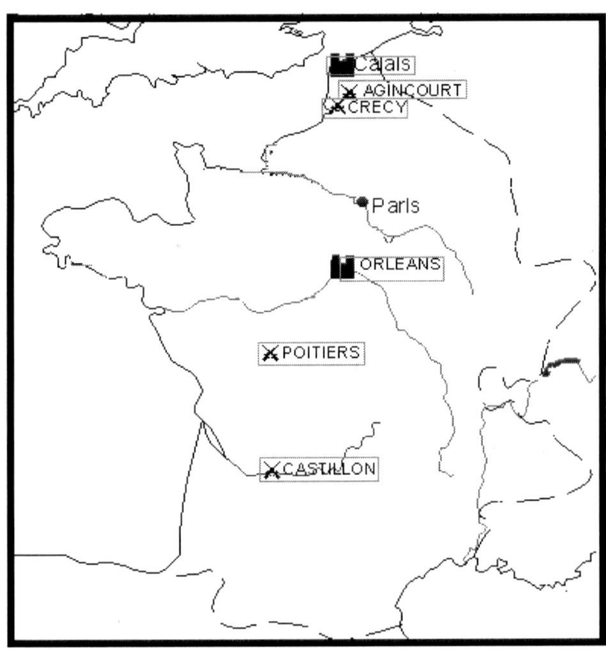

Battle of Crecy (August 26, 1346)
On July 12, 1346, Edward landed an invasion force of about 14,000 men on the coast of Normandy. From there, the English army marched northward, plundering the French countryside. Learning of the Englishmen's arrival, King Philip rallied an army of 12,000 men, made up of approximately 8,000 mounted knights and 4,000 hired Genoese cross-bowmen. At Crecy, Edward halted his army and prepared for the French assault. Late in the afternoon of August 26, Philip's army attacked.

The Genoese crossbowmen led the assault, but they were soon overwhelmed by Edward's 10,000 longbowmen, who could reload faster and fire much further. The crossbowmen then retreated and the French mounted knights attempted to penetrate the English infantry lines. In charge after charge, the horses and riders were cut down in the merciless shower of arrows. At nightfall, the French finally withdrew. Victory at Crecy enabled Edward III of England to lay siege to Calais and force the city defenders to surrender one year later. The battle marked the decline of the mounted knight in European warfare and the rise of England as a world power.

Battle of Poitiers (September 19, 1356)
Son of Edward III of England, Edward the Black Prince, soundly defeated a much larger French army near Poitiers. The French had a number of apparent advantages: they were on home territory, they had many more men (probably around 16,000, twice the size of Edward's force of around 8,000), and they were eager to drive the English out of France because English forces had been at large for years and had pillaged and killed widely. Again, the English longbowmen played the decisive role in the outcome of the battle. The French King John II was captured during the battle and taken to England. He was released in 1360 after he promised to pay an enormous ransom.

Battle of Agincourt (October 25, 1415)
The battle took place in a muddy farmer's field in northern France on October 25, 1415. The two enemies faced one another, exchanging taunts designed to provoke an attack. King Henry V of England marched his force close enough to allow his archers to unleash a hail of arrows upon the French. The French knights charged forward only to be caught in a slippery quagmire of mud. To make matters worse, the French

attackers were unable to effectively swing their broadswords because of the tight quarters of the battlefield and the continuing forward rush of their comrades behind them. Henry's archers fired lethal storms of arrows into this dense mass of humanity until the French began to retreat. The archers then dropped their bows, picked up what weapons they could find and joined the English knights in slaying their foe. The setting sun left a battlefield heaped with the bodies of thousands of French knights and the cream of France's ruling class. The English had dealt their enemy a disastrous blow.

The English, however, failed to achieve a decisive victory in the war which entered into a new phase after the Battle of Agincourt and gradually turned in the French favor.

Drawing of Joan of Arc
by Clément de Fauquembergue
dated 10 May 1429

<u>Lifting of the Siege of Orleans</u> (May 8, 1429)
The siege of Orleans was the turning point of the Hundred Years War. After over 80 years of warfare, the French finally gained the upper hand with the decisive victory at Orleans. Five thousand English troops began the siege of Orleans, the largest fortified position held by Charles VII of France, on October 23, 1428. The siege continued for months. At around this same time, the 17-year-old French peasant girl, Joan of Arc, appears at the court of Charles. Believing that she was following divine guidance, she asked Charles to allow her to lead relief forces to Orléans. Meeting with Joan on March 8, he sent her to Poitiers to be examined by clerics and Parliament. When she returned, Charles permitted Joan to lead a relief force in April. In May, Joan attacked the English in unison with a force from Orleans and drove the English from their positions. The next day the British abandoned the siege; momentum now lay with the French. In 1430, Joan of Arc was captured by the Burgundians who handed her over to the English. She was burned at the stake for heresy in the same year.

<u>Battle of Castillon</u> (July 17, 1453)
In 1451, the French successfully captured Bordeaux from English control. This victory was considered a decisive end of the Hundred Years' War, but the English still considered it their right to reclaim their mainland territories. Consequently, an English army landed on the mainland near Bordeaux in 1452 under the leadership of one of the most famous English mili-tary leaders of the period, John Talbot.

The English forces were able to retake the city of Bordeaux and expanded their control in 1453. It was against this English campaign that French King Charles VII mustered his armies and headed for Bordeaux in mid-1453. On their advance to

Bordeaux, the French army laid siege to the town of Castillon. While besieging the town, the French constructed an extraordinary artillery camp which was heavily fortified and included some 300 guns. This was one of the earliest instances where artillery was used as the primary form of weaponry on a European battlefield. The French camp was further protected by a ditch on one side, palisades on two sides, and a river towards the fourth side.

English leader, John Talbot, had reached the mainland with 3,000 men and reached as many reinforcements later. However, when advancing towards the French camp, he had 500 men-at-arms and 800 mounted archers with him. Rather than waiting for the rest of the English army, John Talbot engaged a small French group of archers and quickly defeated it.

Urged on by this minor victory, the small English army didn't wait for the rest of the army and advanced towards the main body of the French army. The French army, in turn, was well protected by the artillery camp which proved lethal for the English and blew most of the English force under Talbot to pieces. The Battle of Castillon was the last battle between the English and the French as part of the Hundred Years' War. In a sense, this event marked the birth of the French nation-state that would later become known as the nation of France.

Throughout the 1500s France prospered, becoming a center of trade, industry, agriculture, learning and culture. Progress was hampered, though, by religious civil wars between Catholics and Protestant Huguenots, as part of the Reformation.

The 16th century began in France as a time of relative peace, prosperity, and optimism. Horizons soon darkened under the clouds of religious schism, heresy persecutions, and civil war. Catholic French theologians condemned Martin Luther's ideas as early as 1521, but his views continued to spread underground. The movement remained small and clandestine until the 1550s, when Protestant Reformed churches demanded the right to worship openly.

The French monarchy became weak after the accidental death of King Henry II in 1559 which left France with a religiously divided court and a series of young, inexperienced kings. Some powerful noble families wanted to take advantage of this situation to gain more power. In this situation, Catholics were supported by the House of the Guise, while the House of Bourbons sympathized with the Protestants (known as Huguenots).

Henry's widow, Catherine de Medici (a Catholic), attempted a policy of compromise that backfired. Militancy increased on both sides of the religious divide, and civil war broke out. In March 1562, the idea of religious freedom had become too much for the Guise family, and the Duke of Guise led an army against a protestant church in Champagne. The entire congregation, unarmed men, women and children were slaughtered. This was to be the start of almost 40 years of war. During the first three civil wars (1562–63, 1567–68, 1568–70) Catherine de Medici struggled to find a balance between the Catholic and Protestant sides, with some success, and a temporary peace was found in 1570.

But this peace was not to last. Catherine plotted with the Guise family to assassinate a member of the Montmorency-Chatillon family. Montmorency-Chatillons were mostly Catholics who, for political reasons, supported the Protestant causes. But the plot failed and the truth of the attempt soon emerged. A Protestant uprising seemed likely, and to preempt this, Catherine persuaded Charles IX (who ascended the throne of France upon the death of his brother Francis II in 1560) to act first. The most infamous period of the religious wars was about to start.

On August 24, 1572, forces acting for the King executed several thousand Huguenots in Paris in what is now known as the "St. Bartholomew massacre." Lasting several weeks, the massacre expanded outward to other urban centers and the countryside. Modern estimates for the number of dead across France vary widely, from 5,000 to 30,000.

Rarely to this day has such a systematic witch hunt been as rapid and brutal as those few days in 1572. It was also a turning point for the Huguenots. Until that point, they generally were peace-loving people, but quickly became willing to do battle against a church they now saw as being dominated by the devil.

This launched further war, and in response, Catholics formed a Holy League. Their members persuaded Henry III (Henry III, the younger brother of Francis II and Charles IX had taken the throne in 1576) that he should repeal earlier religious freedoms granted to the Huguenots. Inevitably, this led to a further Huguenot uprising.

The bloody warfare that raged within the French kingdom for 36 long years officially ended in April 1598, with the signing of the peace agreement, Edict of Nantes. This treaty was more concrete as compared to all the other peace pacts that were signed previously. It conceded civil rights to the Protestants and granted them freedom to practice their own religion. The Edict also assured equal opportunities in education and public office, to both Catholics and Protestants, and fostered the spread of a movement already underway for the renewal of Catholic spirituality and reform of Catholic church institutions in France.

In the three centuries following Charles VII's reign, many of his successors attempted to expand France's power, as well as their own. The French kings increased their own authority by steadily reducing the power of the nobles, who had long ruled their vast estates like petty kingdoms. Some French kings also pursued a vigorous foreign policy. For example, Francis I, who ruled from 1515 to 1547 CE, waged numerous wars in Europe. In these conflicts, he won control of important Italian territories and initiated a long-standing rivalry between French and German rulers.

France also sponsored voyages of exploration to the recently discovered New World. In the early 16th century, it joined the race to explore the New World and exploit the resources of the Western Hemisphere. In 1534, navigator Jacques Cartier claimed northern North America for France, naming the area around the St. Lawrence River New France. Samuel de Champlain also made great strides for French exploration of the New World. He explored the Caribbean in 1601 and the coast of New England in 1603 before traveling farther north. In 1608 he founded Quebec, and he made numerous Atlantic crossings as he worked tirelessly to promote New France.

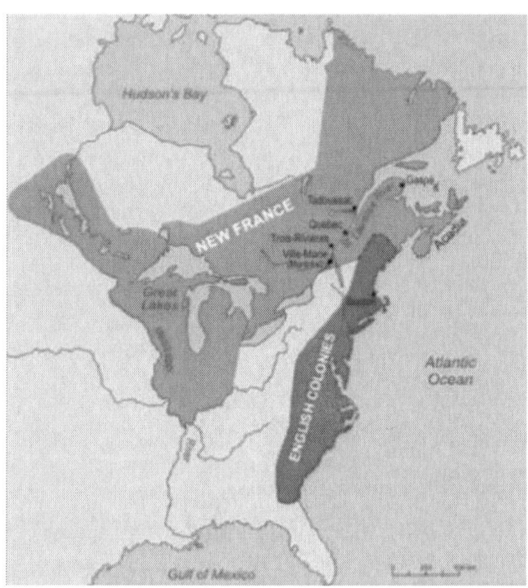

The French were primarily interested in establishing commercially viable colonial outposts, so they created extensive trading networks throughout New France. They relied on native hunters to harvest furs, especially beaver pelts (used to make hats), and to exchange these items for French goods, like glass beads. The French also dreamed of replicating the wealth of Spain by colonizing the tropical zones. After Spanish control of the Caribbean began to weaken, the French turned their attention to small islands in the West Indies. Though it still lagged far behind Spain, France now boasted its own West Indian colonies with lucrative sugar plantation sites and African slave labor.

Louis XIV, The Sun King

Perhaps the greatest French king of all was Louis XIV, known as the Sun King. He ruled from 1643 to 1715, the longest royal reign in European history. Determined to make France the strongest nation on earth, he fought four large-scale wars against other European nations, seized land in Italy and the Netherlands, and set up prosperous trading posts in North America and India. Louis was also a staunch patron of the arts and learning. He established academies of painting and sculpture, science, architecture, and music. He also transformed the royal hunting lodge near Paris into the magnificent Palace of Versailles. Taking nearly thirty years to complete, when finished the palace was so huge it accommodated over 10,000 guests and servants and included a chapel, a theater, and an opera house.

Louis's four wars, building projects, and lavish lifestyle required a great deal of money, most of which came from taxing the peasant class known as the "third estate." France's second estate consisted of the well-to-do nobility, with the Christian clergy making up the first estate. Members of the first and second estates did not pay taxes, which allowed them to enjoy a luxurious lifestyle at the expense of commoners.

This unfair situation became increasingly unbearable and dangerous in the years following Louis XIV's death. His successor, Louis XV, wasted large sums of money on personal luxuries. He also waged costly wars, the most devastating being the French and Indian War in the Americas which lasted from 1756 to 1763. (This war pitted the British against the French and North American Indians.) France was defeated and lost most of its North American colonies.

Louis XV died in 1774, only to be replaced by another weak and selfish king, Louis XVI. Under him, the third estate continued to bear the burden of heavy taxes, causing the treasury to shrink to where by 1787 the country was deeply in debt. Social discontent, which had been building for decades, rose to a breaking point.

The Bastille

Louis then, in 1789, made the mistake of calling a meeting of delegates from each of the three estates. He hoped to squeeze more money out of the third estate. The plan backfired when the delegates suddenly declared themselves to be France's

National Assembly and demanded the King to draft a new constitution. When Louis refused, a mob stormed and captured the Bastille. Serving as a prison, the Bastille had become a symbol of the King's absolute power. The date was July 14, 1789, which the French have celebrated as their Independence Day (Fête Nationale) ever since.

The Revolution, which lasted from May 5, 1789 – November 9, 1799, brought about a new France. Its leaders terminated the feudal system and hereditary privilege, drafted a constitution, drew up a declaration of rights, and established the French Republic. Also, they abolished the church's political power and the monarchy's absolute power.

While Louis XVI was permitted to remain on the throne as a limited monarch, the Revolution took a radical turn. First, Louis was tried for treason and condemned to death by way of guillotine. Nine months later, his wife, Marie Antoinette suffered the same fate. By 1793, the revolutionary government was in crisis. France was being attacked by foreign countries on all sides hoping to restore the monarchy and stop the spread of democratic views. From within, radicals, led by Maximilien Robespierre, took over the government on September 5, 1793, and a dark and violent period of time, known as the Reign of Terror, commenced.

During the Terror, France was ruled by a group of men called the Committee of Public Safety. The Committee introduced several new laws. One of these laws was called the "Law of Suspects." This said anyone who was even suspected as an enemy of the revolution was to be arrested. They then created a court called the Revolutionary Tribunal for the trials. At one point, the court would determine only two verdicts: the accused was either innocent, or guilty and put to death.

Throughout the next year, people had to be careful of everything they said, what they did, and with who they talked. The slightest hint of opposition to the revolutionary government could mean prison or even death. Sometimes revolutionaries accused people they didn't like or wanted to get rid of without any evidence. Over 200,000 people were arrested with around 17,000 people executed. Many more died in prison or were beaten to death in the streets.

As the bloodshed and executions of the Terror became worse, many people realized that it could not continue. Enemies of Robespierre overthrew him on July 27, 1794; the Reign of Terror came to an end when Robespierre, himself, was guillotined.

During the final stage of the French Revolution, the Directory was the name of the government that ruled France. It was in place for only four years from November 2, 1795 to November 10, 1799. The Directory consisted of an executive branch called the "Five Directors" and a legislative branch called the "Corps Legislatif."

The Five Directors acted as the executive branch and were responsible for the day-to-day running of the country. The Corps Legislatif was divided into two houses: the Council of Five Hundred and the Council of Ancients. The Council of Five Hundred proposed new laws and The Council of Ancients voted on the laws proposed by the Five Hundred. Ancients also selected the Five Directors.

When the Directory came into power, it was faced with many problems including widespread famine, civil war, internal corruption, and war with neighboring countries. There was also a struggle for power within the directory between royalists and radical revolutionaries. As the Directory moved from crisis to crisis, the people became unhappy with the new government. The Directory used military force to put down uprisings. They also annulled elections when they didn't like the results.

As the Directory became more and more corrupt, the military leaders of France grew in power. One particular general, Napoleon Bonaparte, had gained many victories on the battlefield. On November 9, 1799, he overthrew the Directory and established a new government called the "Consulate." He established himself as the First Consul and would later crown himself emperor.

Napoleon I

Within three years, he reformed the country's finances, arranged a peace with the Church, and brought the war against France's enemies to a successful, if temporary, conclusion.

With the 1802 Treaty of Amiens, which temporarily ended hostilities between France and the United Kingdom, France became once again the supreme power on the Continent. Two years later, on December 2, 1804, in the cathedral of Notre Dame at Paris, Napoleon took the imperial crown from the hands of Pope Pius VII, whom he had summoned from Rome, and placed it on his own head. Until the final turning point of his fortune, the saga of Napoleon's career is the greatest success story ever told.

Still recognized today for his major achievements, Napoleon instituted religious freedom and an enlightened civil code. The French Civil Code (The Napoleonic Code) was enacted on March 21, 1804. The Code represents a comprehensive reformation and codification of the French civil law and was considered by Napoleon himself to be one of his most significant achievements. Nowadays it remains a strong legal, sociological, and cultural landmark for the French nation. And in spite of some revisions that were introduced later, the Napoleonic code is still very applicable in the French Republic and Law today.

For the next several years, Napoleon led France's armies to victory over the forces of Europe's strongest nations. But in 1815, the allied armies of Britain, Prussia, and Austria entered Paris, exiled Napoleon to the island of Elba, and restored the House of Bourbon to the French throne. However, this was not the last France would hear from Napoleon. After 300 days, Napoleon escaped from Elba, landed in southern Europe and marched on Paris. His brief "Hundred Days" back in power ended with the Battle of Waterloo and his return to exile, this time to the South Atlantic island of St. Helena. At Waterloo,

Bonaparte was defeated by a British-led allied army under the command of the Duke of Wellington, and a Prussian army under the command of Field Marshal Blücher. The battle marked the end of the Napoleonic Wars.

Napoleon Bonaparte died there in 1821, and in 1840 his remains were returned to Paris.

Once power was restored to the House of Bourbon, three fairly ineffective French Kings—Louis XVIII (1815-24), Charles X (1824-30) and Louis Philippe—tried to restore France to the strong monarchy it enjoyed in the past. However, the radicals of the poor working-class who saw the changes brought about by the French Revolution were not willing to return to the old status quo. (The people revolted, once in 1830 and again in 1848, the latter resulting in Louis Philippe's ouster as king.)

The Second Republic in France was established soon after, and elections brought Napoleon's nephew, Louis Napoleon Bonaparte, to the office of president. Two years later, in 1851, Louis Napoleon led a coup d'état and proclaimed himself Emperor Napoleon III. However, Napoleon, who was an ineffective leader, threw glittering parties at the royal palace and vacationed lavishly. To make matters worse, Napoleon involved France in a variety of bloody conflicts, including the Crimean War (1853-56) and the devastating Franco-Prussian War (1870-71), a conflict that ended with Prussia taking Napoleon III prisoner.

◈

The Crimean War (1853-1856) was arguably the most significant conflict of 19th century Europe, setting in place many of the factors that would ultimately lead to the outbreak of the First World War in 1914. The war was fought between the Russians and an alliance of French, British and Ottoman forces, and was designed to stop Russian expansion at the expense of Ottoman territory in the Balkans. The Crimean War was fought mostly in the Crimean Peninsula.

In reality, the French and British were motivated mostly by their own interests rather than any great concern for Ottoman lands. France and Britain, the superpowers of the time, feared Russia's domination of the Black Sea and declared war on Russia in March 1854. The Black Sea was an important part of the trade routes to India and Egypt, thus their interest in protecting it. Another major factor was the dispute between Russia and France over the privileges of the Russian Orthodox and Roman Catholic churches in the holy places in Palestine.

The two great European powers succeeded in their aim, but it was a victory in which the winning side sustained very heavy losses—95,000 French, and 22,000 British soldiers died. The

Crimean War is sometimes called the first "modern" war, since the weaponry and tactics used had never been seen before and affected all other wars thereafter.

The Franco-Prussian War was waged between France and Prussia and the German states from July 15, 1870 to Feb. 1, 1871. Napoleon I had smashed through the German states with ease during the Napoleonic wars. Now a generation later, the roles would be reversed. Even though the war was a short duration, it dramatically changed European history.

From 1868 on, Otto von Bismarck, Chancellor of the North German Confederation, prepared to unite the German Protestant states of the north with the German Catholic south by provoking a war with France. He believed a war would unite the German north and south more quickly than the years or decades it might otherwise take. While the Germans were divided culturally and politically, they were united in their hatred for France since the Napoleonic Wars, when France had looted the German states and forced an estimated 250,000 Germans into the French armies.

In 1869, the throne of Spain was offered to a prince of the Catholic branch of the Prussian Hohenzollern royal family. France learned about the offer and sent an ambassador demanding that Prussia reject it—since France did not want to be surrounded by Hohenzollerns (i.e. Catholics). The Prussian King Wilhelm I sent a telegram assuring the French Emperor, Napoleon III, that the prince would not become king of Spain. Bismarck, as Chancellor of Prussia, publicly released a version of the telegram he edited to make it appear King Wilhelm had insulted Napoleon's ambassador. As Bismarck had hoped, the two sides exchanged angry words, France declared war, and on July 19, 1870 the war started.

The rapid and overwhelming victory of the German states under the leadership of Prussia made possible the creation of a unified German Empire. This then brought the fall of Napoleon III's Empire which was replaced by a provisional government formed by Adolphe Thiers, a French statesman and historian.

Meanwhile, the Germans (Prussians) surrounded Paris and the inhabitants were reduced to virtual starvation. Finally, on January 28,1871 Paris surrendered. In the peace treaty that followed, France lost Alsace-Lorraine and was ordered to pay a war-damage payment. Adding to insult, German troops were stationed in northern France until it was paid.

In the wake of France's defeat, and the terms of the peace treaty, workers and students of Paris joined together to form a revolutionary government called the Paris Commune. Elected on March 26, the Commune was in direct opposition to the conservative national government.

Inspired by the Marxist politics, and revolutionary goals of the International Workingmen's Organization, workers of Paris united to overthrow the existing French regime which had failed to protect the city from Prussian siege. The elected Council of the Commune passed socialist policies and oversaw city functions for just over two months. Then the national government organized its forces and struck back by sending troops into Paris on May 21. In fierce fighting that lasted a week, the Commune government and the people's revolt were destroyed. Perhaps as many as 20,000 Communards were killed, and thousands more were arrested.

Afterwards, Thiers was named president and quickly managed to pay the war-damage payment demanded by Germany. The last German soldiers left France in September 1873. In 1875 the National Assembly established the Third Republic by one vote.

During the 19th century, the economic revolution in France introduced mass manufacturing and railroad building. It also saw the growth of financial institutions with Paris becoming a large European banking center, second only to London.

France rapidly became the world's second leading industrial power, after Great Britain. French manufactured products such as silk, gloves, and porcelain became widely recognized abroad and prized for their high quality.

Modernization of farming also progressed, leading to increased rural prosperity and better nutrition. Running water, gas, electric, and telegraph offices became common in cities. Canals, railways, and roads expanded, and in 1900 the Paris Métro (subway) was open. Factories multiplied in the coal district of the north (steel, chemicals, and automobiles) and around Leon (textiles). A symbol of this prosperity was the erection of Paris's Eiffel Tower (1885-1889), made entirely of steel beams and rivets.

During the period of 1890 to 1914, prosperity increased, as did consumerism. Newspapers became widespread, and both literature and art flourished. With railroads to provide transport, wintertime resort towns in the French Riviera boomed.

In the 20th century, European nations formed competing military alliances. As a result, World War I broke out in 1914 when a Serbian nationalist assassinated Austrian Archduke Franz Ferdinand, the heir to the throne of Austria. The main members of the Allied Powers were France, Russia, and Britain. (France's desire to enter World War I against Austria-Hungary and Germany also stemmed from its desire to regain Alsace and Lorraine.) The United States also fought on the side of the Allies after 1917. The main members of the Central Powers were Germany, Austria-Hungary, the Ottoman Empire, and Bulgaria.

Most of the fighting took place in Europe along two fronts: the western front and the eastern front. The western front was a long line of trenches that ran from the coast of Belgium to Switzerland. The fighting along this front took place in France and Belgium. The eastern front was between Germany, Austria-Hungary, and Bulgaria on one side and Russia and Romania on the other.

Soldiers fighting from a trench

By the end of 1914, both sides had built a series of trenches that went from the North Sea and through Belgium and France. Trench warfare consumed thousands of soldiers as cannon fodder merely to gain a few yards of territory. In fact, neither side gained much ground for three and a half years from October 1914 to March of 1918. They just bombed and shot at each other from across the trenches.

The typical trench was dug around twelve feet deep into the ground. There was often an embankment at the top of the trench and a barbed wire fence. Some trenches were reinforced with wood beams or sandbags. The bottom of the trench was usually covered with wooden boards called duckboards. The duckboards were meant to keep the soldiers' feet above the water that would collect at the bottom of the trench.

The trenches weren't dug in one long straight line but were built as more of a system of zigzag patterns. To say the least, trenches were quite disgusting. There were all sorts of pests living in the trenches including rats, lice, and frogs. The rats were everywhere and got into the soldiers' food and ate just about everything, including sleeping soldiers. The lice were also a major problem. They made the soldiers' itch horribly and caused a disease called Trench Fever.

The weather also contributed to rough conditions in the trenches. Rain caused the trenches to flood and get muddy. Mud could clog up weapons and make it hard to move in battle. Also, the constant moisture could cause an infection called Trench Foot that, if untreated, could become so bad that a soldier's feet would have to be amputated. Cold weather was dangerous, too. Soldiers often lost fingers or toes to frostbite and some died from exposure in the cold.

Some of the major battles during the war included the First Battle of the Marne, Battle of the Somme, Battle of Tannenberg, Battle of Gallipoli, and the Battle of Verdun. Of the eight million French men who served, 1,357,800 were killed and some 4,800,000 were counted as wounded, prisoners of war, or missing.

The fighting ended on November 11, 1918 when a general armistice was agreed to by both sides. The war officially ended between Germany and the Allies with the signing of the Treaty of Versailles. Among its terms included the return of Alsace-Lorraine to France and a war-damage payment of 33 billion dollars from Germany (which German economists calculated would take until 1988 to pay).

The Germans greatly resented the humiliation of the treaty, and this was one of the factors which sparked World War II. During the "Entre Guerres" (Between Wars), France played a leading role in the avant-garde movement, attracting artists, musicians, and filmmakers from around the world.

The decade of relative harmony and compromise between France and Germany came to an end when Adolf Hitler was named the Chancellor of Germany in 1933. At first, France tried to work with the new leader, but when Hitler invaded Poland in 1939, France joined with Britain in declaring war against Germany. Although an ill-prepared force from France tried to subdue the German armies, by June 1940, Nazi Germany occupied three-fifths of France's territory (Northern France and the entire French Atlantic Coast) and on July 10,

1940 established a new French government based at the town of Vichy.

This government was commonly referred to as "Vichy France" and was headed by Henri Philippe Pétain, a General during World War I. Vichy's senior leaders and civilian anti-semites aided in the sending Jews of France to forced labor to Nazi Germany, in particular those of foreign citizenship.

The Nazi German occupation proved costly as Nazi Germany appropriated a full one-half of France's public sector revenue. Furthermore, the Germans appropriated ferrous (containing iron) and non-ferrous metals, bronze statues, zinc, coal, leather, textiles, and chemicals to build and maintain their war machine.

The French who refused defeat and collaboration with Nazi Germany, organized resistance movements in occupied France, Vichy France, and in exile with the support of the UK. Their leader was Charles de Gaulle, Under-Secretary of State for War and National Defense, whose role in the resistance was to pave the way for his immense impact on the future of

France, as leader of its provisional government and first President of the French Fifth Republic.

During the November 8-16, 1942 "Operation Torch," France's Resistance forces joined the Anglo–American invasion of French North Africa. It was aimed at reducing pressure on Allied forces in Egypt and enabling an invasion of Southern Europe. It also provided the second front which the Soviet Union had been requesting since it was invaded by the Germans in 1941.

After four years of occupation and strife, Allied forces, including French Resistance, liberated France in 1944. By the time of the Normandy Invasion, the Free French forces numbered more than 400,000 strong. However, for political reasons, the main French forces which fought in the battle of Normandy landed in France after D-Day. Nine hundred Free French troops were part of the British contingency at Utah Beach. With the assistance of the London-based French Forces, the British Special Operations Executive orchestrated a campaign of sabotage to be carried out by the French Resistance. The Allies developed four plans for the Resistance to execute on D-Day and the following days:

- a 15-day operation to sabotage the rail system
- destroying electrical facilities
- delaying operation aimed at the enemy forces that would potentially reinforce Axis forces at Normandy
- cutting underground telephone and teleprinter cables
- destruction of enemy command posts
- destruction of oil depots

- destruction of ammunition depots

The damage and humiliation suffered by the French at the hands of the Germans was no secret to France's colonies. As the economy in France worsened, the native people of these colonies began to notice they were the ones bearing the brunt of this disaster. In Algeria, a movement for greater autonomy at the beginning of the war turned into an all-out independence movement by the war's end. During the brutal Algerian War of Independence (1954-1962), indigenous rebel attacks led to executions, torture, and untold massacres, which only strengthened the resolve of the Algerian people. In 1962, Charles de Gaulle finally negotiated an end to the war, giving the Algerian people their independence.

General Charles de Gaulle

Following France's liberation in 1944, General Charles de Gaulle was appointed France's Provisional President. However, because he sensed the French people were not in favor of a strong presidency, he resigned soon after in 1946.

The rebuilding of France after the war required a strong central government, whereby most banks, insurance companies, automobile plants, and energy firms fell under government control. Other businesses remained privately operated, the aim being to combine the efficiency of government with the vitality of private industry. Nevertheless, progress was slow, and by 1947 France was forced to turn to the United States for loans as part of the Marshall Plan to rebuild Europe.

One of the goals of the Marshall Plan was to stabilize Europe, both financially and politically, by preventing the expansion of Soviet power and ideals. (The widespread destruction and death, as well as resulting starvation and poverty, made doctrines of Communism appealing to a great many people. Therefore, under the Marshall Plan, the United States offered aid to any country needing it, provided they were not affiliated with Communism.) The Pro-Stalinist members of France's Communist Party found themselves on the losing end of disputes involving American aid, the colonies and workers' demands. As a result, they were expelled from the government with a new constitution, the Fourth Republic, adopted in 1947. Many new industries were institutionalized, such as hydroelectric and nuclear power, oil and gas exploration, chemical refineries, steel production, naval construction, car factories, and building construction. Yet, the Fourth Republic was hamstrung by an ineffective executive branch and the unbearable situation in Algeria. De Gaulle resolved the first of these problems by drafting a new constitution which authorized considerable powers to be given to the President at the expense of the National Assembly. The new constitution became law on October 4, 1958 and the Fifth Republic was born.

French workers and students united in 1968

By the 1960s, with a rise in unemployment and pressure from the anti-authoritarian baby boomers clamoring for social change, France exploded. In May 1968, a protest among students at the university of Nanterre soon spread to the Sorbonne University. Workers also joined the protests. On May 10, the riot police attacked demonstrators, and in response, the trade unions called a general strike across France. De Gaulle took advantage of these events, and just as the country seemed it was on the brink of revolution, reforms were instituted to appease both workers and students.

For three decades following World War II, France experienced greater political stability, a rising birth rate and lowered death rate, and the world's highest economic growth rate. This economic growth involved state economic planning, protectionism, and close cooperation between government, financial institutions, and businesses.

However, from the mid-1960s, France's fortunes were generally less positive than during the previous three decades. A declining birthrate had advantages, but it also lowered consumer demand and thus prosperity. Industrial production declined, unemployment rose, and the OPEC-generated petroleum crisis of 1973-1974 hit France hard. (OPEC is the abbreviation for Organization of Petroleum Exporting Countries, whose members are Saudi Arabia, Iran and Iraq.) France had little domestic oil and imported three-quarters of its petroleum. As a result of this crisis, France elected to develop nuclear power.

For some time, the Fifth Republic's government had been conservative. In 1981, however, the country took a sharp turn to the left. A new socialist president, François Mitterrand, placed major industries, insurance companies, and banks under government control. Increased economic regulation, plus greatly expanded and expensive social service programs, led to monetary inflation (a general increase in prices and fall in the purchasing value of money), low industrial growth, and soaring unemployment. Soon, even many French Socialists sought to replace leftist ideologies decision-making with more of a down-to-earth approach.

The 1980s and 1990s saw dramatic rises in automobile and television ownership, but crime also jumped as unemployment soared to 12%. Rising crime, in turn, stimulated a right-wing, anti-immigrant political backlash, especially under the leadership of Jean-Marie Le Pen. (Le Pen was a French nationalist who represented the main right-wing opposition to the country's mainstream conservative parties from the 1970s through the early 21st century. Le Pen was accused by his opponents of xenophobia and anti-Semitism.)

In 1995, a fairly conservative government under President Jacques Chirac took the presidency back from the Socialist. One trend under Chirac was the continued privatization of most companies nationalized under the Socialists.

Today, France is considered one of the world's most highly developed and well-run nations. France possesses the world's ninth largest economy by Gross Domestic Product (GDP) and Europe's second-largest economy by nominal GDP. In terms of aggregate household wealth, France is the wealthiest nation in Europe and the fourth largest in the world. The citizens of France enjoy a very high standard of living, a superior educational system, and one of the highest life expectancies in the world. Moreover, the World Health Organization (WHO) recently listed France as having the world's "best overall system of health care."

YouTube:
"The Entire History of France in 23 Minutes"

"French Monarchy Family Tree (Charlemagne to Louis Philippe II)"

A Summary of the Five French Republics

• The French First Republic was founded in 1792 and lasted twelve years (1792–1804). It was born out of the French Revolution, which saw the deposition of the Bourbon dynasty and execution of King Louis XVI. This period was characterized by the fall of the monarchy, the establishment of the National Convention, the Reign of Terror, the founding of the Directory, and, finally, the creation of the Consulate and Napoleon's rise to power.

• The French Second Republic was founded in 1848 and lasted four years (1848–1852). French liberals finally displaced the Bourbons for good. French citizens elected Napoleon's nephew, Louis-Napoléon Bonaparte, as France's new President. By 1852, Louis, declared a new French Empire under his regal name, Napoleon III. It officially adopted the motto of the First Republic, *Liberté, Égalité, Fraternité.*

• The French Third Republic was founded in 1870 and lasted seventy years (1870–1940). Following the Franco-Prussian War, Germans invaded and occupied northern France, and Paris fell to a short-lived socialist rebellion (Paris Commune). French politicians convened to restore order and rebuild the military. After World War I, France reclaimed the territory of Alsace-Lorraine. The Nazi invasion of 1940 did away with the Third Republic, replacing it with a collaborationist Vichy regime that lasted through the war.

• The French Fourth Republic was founded in 1946 and lasted twelve years (1946–1958). It was established shortly after the Nazi defeat and sought to reestablish France's presence not just in Europe, but also on the world stage. The Fourth Republic saw an era of great economic growth in France and the rebuilding of the nation's social institutions and industry after World War II. It also saw the beginning of the German-French cooperation that later led to the development of the European Union.

However, the Fourth Republic's weakened executive lacked power to deal with challenges presented by anti-colonial rebellions in Africa and Southeast Asia. While the French suffered military defeats in places like Vietnam, it was the rebellion in Algeria that caused the most disruption. By the late 1950s, the Algerian War appeared less like a colonial revolt and more like a civil war, and in 1958, French officers in Algiers staged a *coup* in order to obtain a more decisive stance from Paris.

• The French Fifth Republic was founded in 1958 and continues to this day (1958–present). Under the constitution crafted by Charles de Gaulle, executive power was increased at the expense of the National Assembly. In 1959 de Gaulle was inaugurated as the first President of the Fifth Republic. In 1962 de Gaulle pushed through a constitutional amendment that provided for direct popular election of the president. In 1965 he became the first French president elected by popular vote since 1848. He was succeeded by Georges Pompidou (1969–74), Valéry Giscard d'Estaing (1974–81), François Mitterrand (1981–95), Jacques Chirac (1995–2007), Nicolas Sarkozy (2007–12), François Hollande (2012–17), and Emmanuel Macron (2017– present).

Basic Facts and Geographic Information

- Population: 67.2 million people live in France (2018)

- Capital: Paris, with 2.2 million inhabitants

- Name: République Française (French Republic)

- Motto: Liberté, Egalité, Fraternité (Liberty, Equality, Fraternity)
It first appeared around the time of the Revolution (1789–1799) and was written into the constitutions of 1946 and 1958.

- Government: Semi-presidential republic

- President: Emmanuel Macron

- Flag: Blue, white and red
The French refer to their flag as the Tricolore (French for 'three colors'). The flag dates from the French Revolution and replaced the flag of the monarchy, which was adorned with the *fleur de lis*.

- Religion: France has been dominated by the influence of the Catholic Church, yet the constitution declares it to be a "secular" country.

- Currency: 1 Euro=$1.11 cents

- France is the most visited country in the world.

• Marianne is the embodiment of the French Republic. She represents the permanent values of "Liberty, Equality, Fraternity."

• National Anthem: La Marseillaise
Only the first verse (and sometimes the fourth and sixth) and the first chorus are sung today in France.

Arise, children of the Fatherland,
The day of glory has arrived!
Against us, tyranny's
Bloody standard is raised, (repeat)
Do you hear, in the countryside,
The roar of those ferocious soldiers?
They're coming right into your arms
To cut the throats of your sons, your women!

To arms, citizens,
Form your battalions,
Let's march, let's march!
Let an impure blood
Water our furrows!

• Due to its six-sided shape, France is sometimes referred to as a hexagon.

• France is about 80% the size of Texas.

• The Gallic rooster (le coq gaulois) is the unofficial symbol of France. The Latin word "gallus" means both "rooster" and "inhabitant of Gaul." Certain ancient coins bore a rooster and gradually the figure of the rooster became the most widely shared representation of the French people.

- The name “France” comes from the Latin Francia, which means land or kingdom of the Franks. As the Roman Empire lost control of Gaul, the Franks rose to power and founded dynasties and cultures that became the basis for modern Europe.

Major Geographic Regions

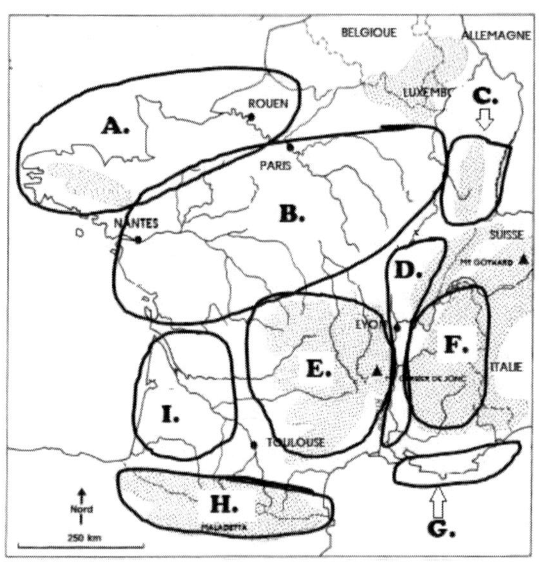

A. The Brittany-Normandie Hills

The low rounded hills and rolling plains of the area are covered with relatively infertile soil. The rugged coastline of Normandy and Brittany is dotted with many bays and is home to both tiny fishing villages and the major seaports of Le Havre and Cherbourg.

B. The Paris Basin

Drained by the Seine, the Paris Basin consists of lowlands of a rich fertile soil. This hilly plain occupies about one-fourth of the country's territory. The Basin, together with southwestern France, is where most of France's grain is produced.

C. The Northeastern Plateaus

These Plateaus are crossed by the Ardennes and Vosges mountain ranges. The lower slopes and valleys are dominated by farms and vineyards. Lorraine has iron and coal deposits in addition to Alsace textile and chemical industries.

D. **The Rhône-Saône Valley**
The river in the north is called the Saône, becoming the Rhône in the south. The region is a major wine-producing area. The town of Lyon has been famous for many centuries for its cooking and production of silk and synthetic fabrics.

E. The Massif Central
High granite plateaus are cut in many places by deep gorges. Extinct volcano cones, known as *puys* (PWEE), are a striking feature of the area. At Vichy, mineral water is bottled for export to distant countries.

F. The French Alps
The Alpine peaks, known as the Massif de Mont Blanc, are crowned by the highest peak in the chain at 15, 771 feet—Mont Blanc. The water from the mountain's streams is harnessed to generate hydroelectric power.

G. The French Riviera
Bordered by the Mediterranean, this region contains many altitudes, from mountains and the charming hill towns down to the coastal plains and sandy beaches. The inland region of Provence-Alpes-Côte d'Azur is characterized by impressive Roman ruins, medieval buildings, ancient olive groves, and even bullfighting arenas.

H. The Pyrenees Mountains
This is a sparsely populated region of the southwest, separating France and Spain. Many of the sheer mountain peaks top 10,000 feet. Farmers raise cattle and sheep on the slopes and foothills.

I. The Aquitaine Basin

This basin supports the Bordeaux wine industry, as well as oil and natural gas fields, steel mills, and chemical factories. Extensive forests, rolling plains, huge sand dunes, and beaches are characteristic features of this area.

Other books in this series:

The 'I Wish I Knew That Before Visiting France' Guidebook

The Celts of Ancient Gaul

Charlemagne: Volume 1: Carolingian Dynasty Rise to Power and the Saxon war

Eleanor of Aquitaine: A Short Biography

The French Resistance: A Brief Introduction

The Life of Josephine Baker and Her 2021 Induction into France's Pantheon

David B. McCoy earned his history teaching degree from Ashland University and his graduate degree from Kent State University. After teaching thirty-two years, David retired to write short books on a wide variety of topics.

Short, concise, and informative, most
Spare Change Press ®
publications are generally
less than 100 pages.

www.amazon.com/author/davidmcco

Made in United States
North Haven, CT
20 March 2025